BEATRICE
and the POGs
By Cory Hills

Copyright© 2018 by Cory Hills

Illustrations by Jane Elliott

AcuteByDesign Publishing

AcuteByDesign.com

ACKNOWLEDGEMENTS

I would like to thank the following people for their amazing assistance, guidance, and support:

Annalise Nawrocki, Sharon Hills, Kelly Niebergall, Jane Elliot, Michel Marion Sharpe, Cathy Saunders, Cynthia MacGregor, and everyone else at AcuteByDesign.

BEATRICE
and the POGs
By Cory Hills

*For Zoie, who once told me that if you want to
see aliens, you had better dream about space!*

"I love it!" exclaimed Beatrice, immediately plopping a bright yellow helmet over her mop of brown hair. Beatrice's parents laughed as they watched her putting on her Chuck Taylors, ready to take her snazzy new bike for a spin.

"Beatrice, it's 7:00pm," began her dad. "It's cold and dark outside. You'll have to wait until morning to ride your bike."

"But it's my birthday," cried Beatrice. "I can't wait!" Her eyes glanced down at her new green bike with its orange seat. The bike still had that fresh-out-of-the-box smell. Tears welled up in Beatrice's eyes. "It's so awesome." Before the tears could fall down her round face, her dad offered a suggestion that would forever change Beatrice's life.

"Well, while we wait until it's light out, why don't you do something with the box the bike came in?" he said, gesturing to the large box sitting alone in the middle of the living room.

"Yeah," added Beatrice's mom, "you're always turning recyclable things into works of art. Just make it one of your projects. I'm sure you can make something fun."

Beatrice gave a couple of sniffles and looked over at the giant box. It did look like a good box to use. It was large, with huge flaps on each side. "I guess I can do that," she sniffled in slight disappointment as she walked over to her art area, which was stuffed to the brim with unfinished projects.

"What can I make?" Beatrice asked herself as she grabbed some markers, pastels, scissors, glue, and paper. She sat down, staring at the brown sides of the box for a good five minutes until her dad popped his head into the room.

"Hey, sweetie, how's it going?"

"Okay," Beatrice said, still moping. "But I can't figure out what to make."

"Hmm," replied her dad. Then with a sly grin he said, "Looks like a spaceship to me! Maybe you could make one and be the first person to fly to Mercury!"

Beatrice laughed. "Yeah right, Dad! Humans have only ever been to the moon."

"Whatever you say, sweetie." He gave her another sly grin and a wink as he left the room. "What was that about?" Beatrice wondered to herself. Her dad was acting weird.

Beatrice looked back at the box and had to admit that her dad was right: the box would make a perfect spaceship! Her face lit up, and for the next hour, she was on a mission to turn the ordinary box into a spaceship. She decorated it as much as she could, both inside and out, using her markers to draw a cockpit, constructing a paper plate steering wheel, cutting out windows, making orange chairs from cracker boxes, and adding other control panels. There were rocket boosters, white wings, and a giant grey engine. Beatrice sat back and admired her work. The spaceship really did look cool.

"Great work, Beatrice!" said her mom when she came into the room. "I knew you could put the box to good use."

"Thanks, Mom," said a proud Beatrice, beaming. "It

came out great!"

"It sure did," replied her mom. "Hey, Beatrice, it's about time for you to brush your teeth and read some books."

"Okay, Mom," groaned Beatrice as she turned back to her spaceship. Beatrice didn't want to get ready for bed. She was too excited about her birthday, her bike, and now her spaceship! It had been an awesome day.

As Beatrice turned away from her mom and back to her spaceship, she thought she caught some movement outside the living room window in the backyard. She tried to look closer, but it was dark outside, and the lights inside made it hard to see clearly outside the window. Just as she stood to get a closer look…

"Beatrice?" called her dad, startling her. She turned toward him.

"Oh! Hey, Dad. You surprised me. Did you happen to see a—"

But her dad ignored her and kept talking. "I have one more present for you. I've wanted to give this to you for a long, long time, but I needed to wait until the right moment. Today, now that you're a big ten-year-old, I think you're old enough for it." He smiled and took out a beautiful silver necklace with a bright orange locket. "You mean everything in the galaxy to me, Beatrice," he said as he handed her the locket.

"Dad, it's so pretty! Thank you!" As she held it in her hand, the locket glittered in the light.

"You are very welcome, my dear. Maybe you can put it in your spaceship to remind you of home when you're off flying through outer space?"

"Oh Dad, it's just pretend!" Beatrice said, laughing, as she leaned inside her spaceship and hung the locket just above the steering wheel.

"Whatever you say, sweetie," he replied with a curious glint in his eyes. "That locket has been in our family for many years and is very special. Take great care of it. It may look like a normal locket, but it's been known to help in times of need." After a brief pause he blurted out, "Books and bed in a few," and left her alone in the living room.

Beatrice laughed to herself. Her dad! He could be such a weirdo. What did he just say? The locket was special? It could help her in outer space? Beatrice shrugged this off. Her dad was always making up crazy stories about space. For as long as she could remember, he had been telling her stories about people from different planets, a gigantic space battle, and spaceships. The stories were very entertaining, and now there was a special locket? Her dad was taking his imagination to a whole new level!

Suddenly, she noticed some more movement in the backyard.

She turned to the living room window, opened the back door, and crept out to the edge of the patio. Had she seen something? An animal? A rabbit? She peered out into the twilight. Nothing. Not even a sound. Beatrice shrugged her shoulders and turned to go back inside.

"Hello," came a voice behind her. "Is that your spaceship inside?"

Beatrice froze and slowly turned. Nothing could have prepared her for what she saw in front of her. Standing there was a girl, but not a human girl. She stood about four feet high with a green, circular face and yellow body. She had two dark eyes, a tiny nose, a large mouth, two huge rabbit-like ears, and two long antennae poking straight out of her head. A mask sat partially on her face.

Beatrice swallowed and said, "Umm—hi…. Err—umm —yes, that's my spaceship. I made it today. Umm—who are you?"

The girl smiled. "My name is Samma." Her voice was sweet but also strong. She seemed friendly.

"Okay," hesitated Beatrice. "My name is Beatrice. Nice to meet you, Samma. Who exactly are you, and what are you doing in my backyard?"

Samma smiled. "I am a space alien. My spaceship crashed, and I need to borrow yours to help me get back to space."

Beatrice's eyebrows raised high on her head. "I'm not sure what you're talking about. I mean, I'd love to help you, but it's my bedtime, and my mom and dad need me. Besides, my spaceship is only made out of cardboard. It isn't even real."

"Beatrice!" came a voice from inside the house. "Time for books and bed!"

"Sorry," stammered Beatrice. "I have to go. Good luck finding your way back to space." Beatrice gave a hesitant wave and turned to walk inside, looking back one more time at Samma.

Samma stood there watching and gave a smile. "Bye, Beatrice," she said and disappeared into the bushes in the backyard.

Beatrice　　　Samma

That night, Beatrice couldn't sleep. She tossed and turned and tossed some more, thinking about Samma, the spaceship, the locket, and her birthday. What a weird night! Had she imagined the whole thing? And what was going on with her dad? At about 2:00 in the morning, Beatrice couldn't take it anymore. She kicked off her covers and leaped out of bed, determined to get some answers.

Once in the narrow hallway, she could see a neon glow coming from the living room. Beatrice thought her dad had left the television on. Again. But when she turned the corner, Beatrice gasped and froze. There in the living room sat her spaceship, blinking a rainbow of colors. "What's going on?" Beatrice whispered aloud. Always the brave one, Beatrice crept closer to the spaceship, determined to find out.

Just then, Samma appeared from within the spaceship and smiled at Beatrice.

"Hello again, Beatrice."

This time Beatrice wasn't as shocked. "Hi, Samma," said a relieved Beatrice. "It's actually nice to see you. I thought I had imagined the whole thing!"

Samma stepped in front of Beatrice and held out her hand. "I assure you I am real."

Beatrice looked down at Samma's yellow hand. Was this really happening? Beatrice reached out and shook Samma's hand confirming that yes, this was real. Beatrice's eyes lit up.

"Wow!" she exclaimed out loud.

Samma smiled. "Beatrice, it is really nice to finally meet you."

"Finally?" asked Beatrice.

"Yes," replied Samma. "We have been looking for you!"

Beatrice furrowed her brow. "Who exactly are *we*?"

"Oh, right!" Samma said, laughing. "Would you like to meet the others?"

"Others?!" asked Beatrice, incredulously. "Other *what*?"

"Aliens, silly!" Samma said with a laugh. "Come with me," and Samma stepped inside the cardboard box spaceship. "Watch your head."

Beatrice stood alone in the living room as Samma disappeared inside the cardboard box spaceship. For a fleeting moment, she thought about turning around and going back to bed. This had to be a dream. But then Beatrice looked at her spaceship and gave a little chuckle. It really did look good. She had put in a lot of work decorating and designing, so Beatrice thought she might as well see what the inside looked like!

She took a deep breath and ducked her head under the flap that served as the entrance. After Beatrice entered, the world transformed. It was enormous! The ship had wide hallways and tall ceilings. And the activity! The spaceship seemed alive: lights were blinking, machines were beeping, and people were moving about.

"Wait a second," Beatrice thought to herself as a tall blue person walked by in the hallway. "Who are these people? Maybe a better question is *what* are these people?"

"Okay, everyone, gather around," announced Samma. Beatrice watched in amazement as six other aliens stepped into line.

Samma continued, "Everyone, this is Beatrice. She built this ship and possesses special powers to help us get back into outer space."

"Special powers?" began Beatrice, but before she could finish, everyone erupted into cheers, clapping and patting each other on the back.

Samma smiled and raised her hand. Everyone hushed. "We have lots of work to do before takeoff, but first let's introduce ourselves to Beatrice. This is a lot for her to take in, so please, let's all be patient and respectful."

One by one, Beatrice met the other aliens—each, as it turned out, from a different planet in the galaxy.

"Hey, Beatrice!" said Rala, a purple alien from Mercury, with two spiraling green ears, thin arms and legs, three eyes, and a blue circle on her chest. The blue circle seemed to pulse darker and lighter as Rala breathed. Her eyes were bright blue and could each move in different directions.

"A heartfelt welcome from Venus," said Samma, with her trademark smile.

"What's up?!" said Keena, a very tall, yellow alien from Mars, with four elbows and a large and bright green star on his chest. His eyes were big, and he had extremely long, pink ears with two small, green stars on each end. The two smaller stars moved by themselves and almost looked like robots sitting on Keena's head.

"Hi," came a very soft voice from Padinny, the smallest

9

alien, from Jupiter, with short legs, thin ears, and five red Xs across her chest. Padinny was so small that her legs were barely longer than Beatrice's forearm. The Xs were a very vivid red, and Beatrice couldn't stop staring at them.

"Hey, hey, hey!" said Graniten, a very tall silver and blue alien from Saturn, with no nose, two long antennae, and two yellow ice skates on his feet. He looked like a figure skater. Beatrice thought to herself, "That makes sense. Saturn has many rings, so maybe he moves around the rings on his skates!"

"Great to meet ya!" exclaimed Cannie, a white alien from Neptune, with four ears, four eyes, and blue hands. Cannie was very peculiar-looking, as each of his eyes and ears was a different color: red, blue, orange, and purple. There were three fingers on each of his blue hands.

"Hello," said an angry-looking Jana, a multi-colored and striped alien from Uranus, with huge eyes, and hands with three fingers.

"Jana certainly wins the award for most colorful space alien!" thought Beatrice to herself. And Jana really was colorful, like a rainbow wrapped around a person.

Beatrice stared in amazement. The names were unique enough, but the physical appearances of the aliens were incredible! Before Beatrice had a chance to process what she was seeing, hearing, and witnessing, she felt dizzy and fell over. Samma caught her and sat her in a white and orange chair.

"Beatrice," she said. "Are you okay? I know this is a lot to take in."

Samma handed Beatrice a glass with a neon orange liquid inside. "Here, drink this." Beatrice looked at the strange liquid. It smelled sweet, kind of like pumpkins. She took a small sip; the color immediately rushed back to her face, and her eyes widened.

"This is delicious! What is it?"

Samma smiled. "It's called Galla. My mother makes it for me during hot summer nights on Venus to cool me down." Samma got a faraway smile on her face and paused before going on. "I'm happy you like it. When we go to Venus, you can meet my mom and tell her you enjoyed Galla!"

Beatrice smiled and then looked confused. "Wait— we're going to Venus? But how?"

The other aliens laughed and started going back to work around the spaceship.

Samma smiled, sat down next to Beatrice, and folded her yellow hands in her lap. "Oh, Beatrice, there is so much to tell you. I promise I will tell you everything, but before that, we need your help."

"Okay," said Beatrice, "what do you need?"

"We need to open your locket."

"What?" asked Beatrice.

"Your locket," repeated Samma. "The one you put in the spaceship above the steering wheel."

Beatrice turned and looked at the steering wheel. There, above it, hung her new locket. "Why do you need to open my locket? It's just something my dad gave me for my birthday."

"It's not an ordinary locket, Beatrice," said Samma. "In fact, it is very special."

Beatrice continued to look doubtful. "Special? How? I mean, I just got it tonight. In fact, I've never even opened it before!"

Samma froze and stared at Beatrice. "You mean you don't know what's inside?"

"Umm … no," Beatrice replied, eyes widening. "What *is* inside?"

Samma took Beatrice's hand in her yellow hand. Someone took Beatrice's glass and refilled it with Galla.

Beatrice looked up. "Thank you, er …?"

"Keena," he said. "I'm Samma's cousin.

Beatrice smiled up at Keena. A boy alien? Samma's cousin? This was getting stranger by the minute!

Keena sat down next to Samma. "Have you told her yet?" he asked Samma.

"I was just about to," replied Samma.

Keena   Cannie

"Tell me what?" asked Beatrice, nervously fidgeting in her seat.

Samma patted Beatrice's shoulder. "Beatrice, what I'm about to tell you may sound a little crazy, but I promise you that it is all true."

"Okay," Beatrice said tentatively.

Samma gestured around her. "We are all space aliens, each one of us from a different planet in the galaxy, chosen by our host planets to be part of a special team that explores and protects the galaxy. We are the POGs, the Protectors of the Galaxy."

Beatrice looked at Samma, then at Keena. Beatrice looked up at Samma's green face and Keena's yellow face, both staring intently at her. After a long pause, Beatrice asked, "How were you chosen? And why were you in my backyard?"

"Both excellent questions," replied Samma. "Keena, would you like to explain?"

Without saying a word, Keena stood up in front of Beatrice. He stretched a bit and then touched the star on his chest with the two stars on his two long ears. All of a sudden there was a flash, and the two stars were on fire, and the whole outside of Keena's body was glowing in flames.

"Whoa," said Beatrice staring at Keena.

Keena touched his two ears together and shot a thin fireball across the room and through a wooden table,

15

creating a perfect hole that simmered and smoked.

"*Ahh*!" shrieked Beatrice, jumping back from her chair.

"Keena," yelled Samma, "don't scare her!" Samma turned to Beatrice. "Sorry about that. Keena likes to show off."

Keena shrugged and winked.

Samma ignored Keena and went on. "He isn't dangerous at all," she assured Beatrice. "Keena, please tell her."

Keena touched the star on his chest with his ears, and just like that, the flames went out, the fiery glow around his body disappeared, and he was back to normal. Keena sat down and took a sip of Galla before explaining. "Beatrice, all of us have special powers—powers that are unique to our planet. I am from Mars, and I can produce fire from my ears and cover myself in a protective flame that serves as a kind of shield."

"Shield for what?" asked Beatrice.

"Well," said Keena getting a proud look in his eyes, "I need a shield when we are battling the—"

"What Keena is saying," interrupted Samma, "is that each of us on this ship possesses a special power."

"Do all the aliens on Mars have the same power you have?" asked Beatrice.

Keena's pink ears stood up straight, and he smiled. "Nope! As far as I know, I am the only one. That's what makes me sooooo cool." Keena held out his long arm to offer a high five to Beatrice. Beatrice smiled and lightly tapped Keena's hand.

"That's enough for now," interrupted Samma suddenly. I think that explains things pretty well."

16

Keena shrugged and said, "Okay, cousin, whatever you say."

Beatrice could see that there was more to this story, but before she could ask, Keena said, "Oh, hey, you should see what Samma can do!"

"I'd rather not," said Samma quietly.

Keena casually pushed Samma's shoulder. "Come on, show her."

"Keena," said Samma with a worried look in her eyes.

"It's okay," interjected Beatrice. "You can show me later if you'd like."

Samma sighed. "Thank you, Beatrice, but it's all right. I'll show you." Samma closed her eyes. She raised her arms, and the palms of her hands began to glow bright white. Suddenly millions of colored dots of light appeared around the room. With the twists and turns of her hands, Samma made the dots move this way and that. Beatrice's eyes grew bigger and bigger as an image began to appear from the colored dots of light. It was an exact picture of Beatrice!

Beatrice was mesmerized. "How did you do that?" Beatrice stepped up and slowly reached her finger out to one of the colored dots of light. The light was similar to sunlight but a bit thicker, grainier. Then just like that, Samma lowered her hands, opened her eyes, and everything disappeared.

"Whoa," said Beatrice.

"Pretty cool, huh?" asked Keena, smiling, sitting back in his chair. "That's my cousin for you!"

Samma blushed.

"How did you do that?" asked an astonished Beatrice.

"Since I am from Venus, I can manipulate gases," began Samma. "Everything in the galaxy is made up of gases, most of which we cannot see. I can sense all the gas molecules in the air around us and move them."

"This really comes in handy when we are..." began Keena, but he trailed off quickly after he saw the look Samma was giving him. "Um, er, it is a really cool power, cousin!"

"That is so cool! All of you have powers," said Beatrice. Then Beatrice lowered her head sadly. "If all of you have such cool powers, why are you here in my living room? Why do you need me? I have no powers. I'm just a kid!"

Samma and Keena both giggled.

Beatrice couldn't understand why they were laughing. "What's so funny?" she asked.

Samma chuckled and Keena snorted at the same time. "We are all kids, silly!"

Beatrice's jaw dropped open. "Wait, what? But Keena is so—"

"Super tall!" interrupted a grinning Keena, standing up and stretching up to the ceiling. "It's true that some of us may look different or appear older, but remember that each of us comes from a different planet. And while we all look different, we are all kids!" At that, Keena touched his ears together and shot a flame across the room that struck Cannie in the elbow.

"Hey!" shouted Cannie with a mischievous grin on his face. "Stop that!" Cannie clapped his blue hands together and fired back an ice pellet that Keena deflected with one of his ears.

"Ha!" retorted Keena.

"Oh, okay, okay!" scolded Samma. "That's enough, you two!" They all laughed and went back to work.

Samma sat down next to Beatrice and smiled. "As you can see, we are a normal group of kids with a big job: protecting the galaxy."

Beatrice thought for a moment. "I still don't understand how I fit in. Why is my locket so important?"

Samma took a deep breath. "Not long ago, we received a special message from space that said you had been chosen to join us."

"**W**hat?!" exclaimed a surprised Beatrice.

"Yes," said Samma. "You are the chosen POG from Earth! After we received the message, we set course for Earth, but right before we entered Earth's atmosphere, the Bracas appeared out of nowhere and shot our ship down. Fortunately, we managed to land safely, and we continued our journey straight to your backyard, where you saw me tonight!"

Beatrice looked perplexed. "Wait—Bracas?"

Samma gave a laugh. "Oh right, sorry! The Bracas are our sworn enemies. As I said earlier, we are the POGS, the protectors of the galaxy, and we protect the galaxy against the Bracas."

Keena sighed and looked up at the ceiling. "The Bracas are not cool."

"Oh," said Beatrice with a confused look on her face.

Samma went on. "The Bracas want to take over the galaxy."

"How could they do that?" Beatrice asked.

"If they collect all the power buckets, then they will be in total control of each planet. We do not want that to happen!"

Beatrice's head began to spin. "Power buckets?"

Keena leaned in. "I'll take this one, Samma. Beatrice, you know how cars and planes on Earth need fuel to move?"

"Yes," replied Beatrice. "We usually use gasoline

for that."

"Exactly," said Keena. "Think of power buckets as a kind of galactic gasoline. In order for aliens to travel throughout the galaxy, they need power buckets for their spaceships. The Bracas want to collect all the power buckets in the galaxy. In doing so, they would control alien movement on every planet in the galaxy! That would be very bad news." Keena leaned back in his chair.

"Cool," said Beatrice, "So you guys, the POGs, make sure the Bracas don't get the power buckets. Well, where are these power buckets?"

"That is precisely the question," replied a very excited Samma. "I believe that the answer lies inside your locket!"

Beatrice glanced over at her locket dangling above the steering wheel in the cockpit. "How?"

"I don't know. Maybe it's your power, silly!" Samma grabbed the locket and handed it to Beatrice. "Open it and find out!"

"I don't know," said Beatrice with a doubtful look on her face. "I mean, this is amazing, and you all seem really nice, but I'm just a normal kid. Also, it's way past my bedtime," she added as if she were in trouble.

Samma listened carefully, then said, "I'll tell you what. Just open the locket and see what happens. If nothing happens, we will leave you alone, and you'll never hear from us again. If something does happen, we'll let you decide what to do."

Beatrice paused for a few moments, ran her fingers through her hair, and straightened her shoulders. "Okay," she finally said. "Let's do it."

"Wonderful!" exclaimed Samma. "Whenever

you're ready."

Beatrice grasped the orange locket in her right hand and stared intently at it. "What am I doing?" she thought to herself. "What if it doesn't work? What if it does? I don't know what to do!"

Just then, Beatrice noticed that all the beeping sounds and murmuring voices had stopped. All the POGs had gathered around the table, gazing hopefully at Beatrice.

Beatrice mustered all the courage she had and said, "Here goes." She grasped the locket with two hands and pried it open. Then she froze, holding it open in her hands.

Nothing happened.

After a few moments, the POGs let out a collective sigh of disappointment. Beatrice looked sadly at Samma. "I'm sorry I couldn't help, Samma." Beatrice stood up and turned to leave the spaceship.

"Wait!" cried Samma in a voice that caused everyone to halt. "It's a locket, which is a kind of necklace, right? Why don't you try wearing it around your neck?"

"I don't know," moaned Beatrice.

"Just try!" said Samma. Samma had such a hopeful look on her face that Beatrice knew she had to at least try.

Beatrice shrugged. "Okay," she said, and she carefully pulled the chain over her head. As soon as the locket fell in front of her chest, a beautiful stream of light burst out of the locket. The light was a vivid, warm white. It wasn't warm like a fire, but rather warm like a good feeling inside you. Beatrice stood there in complete amazement as the steady stream of fantastic light radiated from the locket on her chest.

"Whoa!" shouted Keena.

"Oh my," said Cannie.

"Nice!" offered Graniten.

"Wow," managed Beatrice, staring ahead in wonder.

Samma said nothing. She just smiled – a very satisfied smile.

"What does it mean?" asked Beatrice as she studied the beautiful light pouring out of the locket.

"I don't know," said Samma.

"They appear to be different rays of light," offered Keena. "Do they form something?"

Everyone started talking at once, offering more ideas and suggestions for what the light meant. Suddenly, a quiet voice from the back of the room said, "I know what they are." Nobody seemed to hear. They all kept talking. "Hey, I know," said the voice again, still too quiet. Finally, the voice yelled, "I *know*!"

Padinny

Everyone turned to see who had yelled. All eyes turned to Padinny. She was so small that each POG had to lean in to hear her. Keena actually kneeled down to be closer. Beatrice was mesmerized by the 5 X's across Padinny's chest.

Once Padinny had everyone's attention, she cleared her throat and said quietly, "It's a map."

"A what?" asked Cannie, cupping all four of his ears in his blue hands.

"A map," repeated Padinny, this time a bit more assertively.

"What?! How?" asked Keena.

"No way," said Jana with her arms crossed.

"Beatrice," instructed Padinny in an even voice, "please move over to your right and direct the light onto the black screen on the wall."

Beatrice did as she was told.

"Now Cannie, please project a map of the galaxy onto the screen."

Cannie hit some buttons on what looked like a wrist watch. All of a sudden, light projected from his wrist, and he guided it onto the black screen.

Everyone gasped. The light from the locket pointed out very specific coordinates on the map, and in big, bold letters at the top of the screen read the words *MAP OF POWER BUCKETS.*

"No way!" shouted Keena.

"Amazing!" said Graniten as he skated around the room.

"Hmm," said Jana.

Beatrice felt uneasy. She looked at Padinny. "What does it mean?"

Samma stood up and proudly faced everyone in the room. "Everyone, it appears that Beatrice's locket provides us with a map to find the remaining power buckets in the galaxy!"

Before Beatrice could respond or ask any questions, the room burst into cheers. The POGs were all so excited. Cannie and Keena hugged. Graniten and Jana bumped elbows. Beatrice's eyes grew to the size of grapefruits. "How is this possible?!" she said out loud, staring at the lights emanating from her locket.

Samma put her hand on Beatrice's shoulder and said, "This confirms it. You are one of us, Beatrice. You are the newest POG!" There were hoots, hollers, laughs, jumps, and even some fireballs and ice pellets being shot around. Everyone was ecstatic.

One by one, in order of planet, the other members of POG came up to Beatrice.

"Hey, Beatrice!" said Rala.

"Welcome," smiled Samma.

"Cheers!" shouted Keena.

"Hi," whispered Padinny, peeking up at Beatrice.

"Glad you're here," said Graniten.

"Wahoo!" cried Cannie.

"Hello," said Jana, flatly, peering at Beatrice with a suspicious look in her eye.

Beatrice was speechless, and her cheeks were flushed.

She carefully closed the locket, and the lights disappeared. "Thank you, everyone," began Beatrice. "I am excited to meet you all and be a member of, umm, POG." Beatrice continued slowly. "This is a lot to take in, and my family is asleep in the other room. I need to go talk to them before leaving with you in the spaceship."

Loud gasps could be heard. Beatrice looked out at seven blank faces with extremely disappointed looks on them.

"Calm down, everyone," declared Samma. "Can't you all remember your first night on the ship?"

Cannie laughed, "Yeah, I remember Keena crying all night long!"

Keena punched Cannie's arm. "I wasn't crying, man! I have allergies."

Everyone laughed. Samma smiled and turned to Beatrice. "I'm sorry I haven't explained everything, Beatrice, but as POGs, we possess a special collective power – the power to stop time. We can go on a mission to anywhere in the galaxy, return, and it's as if no time has passed."

"Oh," said Beatrice, curiously.

"Also, we only fly at night. That's how we operate as a group. Right now, your parents are getting your brother to bed in the other room, and when we come back from space they will be in the same place they are in now!"

"Wow!" exclaimed Beatrice, raising her eyebrows, "This is so amazing and unbelievable!"

"Of course, it is!" replied a very excited Keena.

"Sure, it is, whatever," said Jana, squinting her eyes at Beatrice.

"I'm sorry?" asked Beatrice, looking at Jana with a confused face. Jana was the most unique-looking alien because of the dozens of rainbow stripes all over her body.

Samma stepped over and stood in front of Beatrice. "Jana," said Samma in a stern voice, "is there a problem here?"

The room went quiet. Jana rolled her huge eyes and crossed her arms. "No problem," replied Jana in a snarky tone. "Just curious to see if Ms. Locket Girl here is on our side, or if she's leading us into a trap set by the Bracas!"

"Jana," began Rala, "come on."

Beatrice's mouth hung open, and she felt paralyzed. She didn't know what to say. Luckily, Samma did.

"Jana, you have every right to be skeptical, but we have followed proper POG protocol. Beatrice is on our team, and her locket contains valuable information. We mustn't lose sight of the mission."

Jana stared at Beatrice for a while, and then unfolded her arms.

"I guess," she said, "but I'll be watching you." Jana walked out of the room and down the hall.

"Yeah, with her big eyes," joked Keena, and he, Cannie, and Graniten burst into laughter.

Beatrice looked frightened and held very still. "Beatrice?" asked Samma, snapping her out of it. "Don't worry about Jana. She is a very protective alien."

"Okay," replied Beatrice.

Samma went on. "This is a lot for everyone to take in – you, me, and the POGs, – so let's take it slowly. One mission at a time, okay?"

"That sounds good," said Beatrice. "I think I can do

that." Beatrice took a deep breath and rolled her shoulders around. "Well then, what *is* the first mission?"

"Let's go get some power buckets!" said Samma with a smile. "We need to test the accuracy of Beatrice's locket in a place we are all very comfortable going."

Rala's face lit up. "I know a place!" she said excitedly.

"Me, too," shouted Graniten.

Samma paused, smiled, and looked up at everyone. "POGs, I think it's time to go back to school!"

Rala   Graniten Jana

R̲ala jumped up and burst into thousands of little light particles. All the POGs cheered!

"What school?" asked Beatrice.

Rala reappeared from the light and said excitedly, "SEAK! S̲chool for the E̲ducation of A̲lien K̲ids. It's the greatest place in the galaxy! It's where we all met for the first time during our training. And it's on Mercury, my planet! You're going to love it, Beatrice!" Rala turned to Samma. "I'll send a message to Jobu to let her know we will be coming."

"Good idea," said Samma. "Please also let her know we found the POG from Earth!"

"Who's Jobu?" asked Beatrice.

"Oh, Jobu," said Rala, grinning, "is only the wisest alien in the galaxy. She was our teacher and is responsible for us being POGs."

"She's also seriously cool," added Graniten as he zoomed by in his yellow skates.

"Hey Rala?" asked Beatrice as Rala hit a few buttons on her wrist watch. "What's your power?"

Rala finished what she was doing and looked up. "You know how Samma can manipulate gases? Well, I can manipulate light."

"That sounds cool," said Beatrice. "Would you mind showing me?" asked Beatrice.

"Sure!" Rala said before she closed her eyes. The blue circle on her chest began to pulse faster and burst into thousands of multi-colored light particles. The light seemed to just sit in the air as if it were floating.

Beatrice stared around her in amazement. "Wow," she said, "it's beautiful."

Cannie smiled and said, "But wait, there's more! Watch what else she can do."

All of a sudden, Rala lifted her hands, and the light particles began flying around until they settled into the back right corner of the room. With a giant flash, the light disappeared, and there sitting in the corner was a wrist watch, just like the one that Cannie and Rala had.

"What?!" Beatrice yelled aloud, shocked at what had happened.

Rala picked up the watch and handed it to Beatrice. "Since you are a POG, I thought you should have one of these. It's a POG-Watch – a small, computerized wrist watch that Padinny made for all of us."

"Thanks!" exclaimed Beatrice as she slipped the smooth white watch over her wrist. "How did you do that?"

Rala smiled. "I can turn light particles into physical shapes by manipulating the light around me."

"That is absolutely amazing," gushed Beatrice.

"It's all right," said Rala scrunching up her face. "I mean, it does have its drawbacks. I can only use the light that is present in the atmosphere, so my powers are much weaker on planets farther away from the sun." Rala turned to Samma. "All set, Samma. I messaged Jobu and told her we are on our way."

"Thank you, Rala," responded Samma. "I believe it is time for us to launch this ship and look for some power buckets!"

Beatrice sat there thinking. "Hey Samma, how exactly are we going to test my locket?"

"That's a great question, Beatrice. I've been thinking about that, and, to be honest, I was hoping Jobu could help us figure it out. I know we could pick any location from the coordinates provided, but we want to be careful in case this is a trap."

Beatrice turned red. "A trap?"

Samma smiled. "I wouldn't worry about it, Beatrice. I trust you. But if I have learned anything over the years, it is to be careful. Let's see what Jobu says."

Padinny stepped up and said, "Sorry to interrupt, but I have an idea. What if we compare the map coordinates from Beatrice's locket to the coordinates of SEAK? Then we can pick a location that is closest to the school and go check it for power buckets."

"Great idea, Padinny," replied Samma. "That way we are closer to an area we are already familiar with." Samma paused. "Let's set up an exploratory team to survey the area once we reach SEAK and talk with Jobu."

Beatrice sat there and looked over at Padinny. She was so small, yet so confident. "Padinny is really smart!" Beatrice thought to herself. "I guess you can be small and really strong!"

Beatrice was snapped out of her thoughts by a suddenly in-charge Samma.

"Cannie, set course for Mercury. Rala, monitor contact with Jobu. Keena, please check the engines and report back with updated levels of power buckets."

Samma smiled and sat down in the captain's chair just

behind the steering wheel from which the locket had previously hung. "Let's go to Mercury!"

Beatrice sat quietly in a comfortable orange chair, staring outside a spaceship window into her living room. She spotted her new bike standing in the corner of the living room, waiting to be ridden. Beatrice smiled. "I'll ride you tomorrow!" she thought.

Graniten yelled, "Rockets igniting in 3-2-1!"

The rockets blasted, and the ship began to move ahead toward the fireplace, slowly at first and then faster and faster. Beatrice felt a little nervous, the closer they got to the fireplace. When they were just inches away from it, Keena pulled a lever, the fireplace swung open, and the ship sprang through the fireplace and launched up the chimney, shooting out the top in a burst of sparks.

Beatrice's eyes were wide in amazement as her house got smaller and smaller. She was going to outer space! The gravity of the situation had not fully hit her as she sat there with space aliens running around, hitting buttons, and shouting orders. In a matter of seconds, they broke through Earth's atmosphere into outer space.

"Wow!" exclaimed Beatrice, looking out the window at her first glimpse of space. It was absolutely breathtaking.

Samma smiled. "Beatrice, you haven't seen anything yet. Look out the other window."

Beatrice turned around just in time to see the moon! It was so big up close, and the craters were enormous, much bigger than she had thought they would be. The craters were rocky and looked more like tall mountains than the flat circles Beatrice saw on Earth when she looked through a telescope. Beatrice laughed as she looked at the moon.

"What's so funny?" asked Samma.

Beatrice said, "When I was younger, my dad would push me on the swings at our playground. I would tell him to push me higher and higher, and so he did, telling me that he had pushed me all the way up to the moon. He then asked me to bring back some stinky cheese for him, since it's a well-known joke on Earth that the moon is made of cheese. Well, now I know the truth! I guess the moon isn't made of cheese after all!"

Samma smiled. "Your dad sounds funny," she said.

"Oh, he's a complete dork," replied Beatrice with a sweet smile. "He's always telling bad jokes, doing silly dances, and making up the craziest stories about space."

"I bet he would love to see you now!"

Beatrice laughed out loud. "He definitely would!" Then Beatrice remembered the locket he had given her. "Hey, Samma, you know what's interesting?"

"What?" said Samma.

"My dad gave me this locket tonight and after he gave it to me, he made a joke about how I might be able to use it in space. Hmm."

"What are you thinking?" asked Samma.

"I don't really know," replied Beatrice as she held the locket gently in her hand. It looked small against her hand and felt cold against her skin. The locket itself was no bigger than a coin and was a perfect sphere. "It just seems highly unusual."

"I don't know…" trailed off Samma. "Hey, how are you doing with all of this?"

Beatrice took a deep breath. "Okay, I think," she said, laughing. "Well, actually it's been a little overwhelming, but I'm starting to understand more. It's just a lot to take in." Beatrice gestured to her window. "This morning I was on Earth celebrating my tenth birthday with my family, and now I'm in outer space! My head is a little jumbled, but I can't wait to meet Jobu."

Samma smiled. "I promise you will love her, and she will make you feel very comfortable with everything that is going on."

Samma turned her head to look out of the spaceship. "Hey look out your window!"

Beatrice looked out just in time to see a shooting star fly by the spaceship. "Wow!"

Beatrice sat back in her orange chair and stared off into space. She thought about her day. For starters, she had turned ten, got a new bicycle, ate lots of cake – a delicious yellow cake with chocolate icing! But she also discovered that she was a member of a group called POGs – kids like her from each planet with different powers, all trained at a school called SEAK, with the sole purpose of protecting power buckets from being stolen by the evil Bracas. *Phew!*

Beatrice's head felt like it was going to explode. Was this real? Was it a dream? She reached down and pinched her arm.

"Ouch!" she cried out.

"What's that?" asked Samma. "Everything okay?"

"Oh, yeah, sorry," stuttered Beatrice. "I was just thinking about today. It's been quite the birthday!"

Samma walked over and put a hand on Beatrice's shoulder. "I know this is confusing, exciting, frightening, amazing – all in one. Just trust me, Beatrice. You are where you need to be, and Jobu will be able to help explain everything. She is the wisest alien I've ever met."

Beatrice smiled and sighed. "Thanks, Samma, for everything."

"No problem," replied Samma as she turned back to the front window of the spaceship. "Look!" she said. "Venus!"

Beatrice glanced up and saw another planet for the first time. It was stunning. While she could definitely see flames and fires from above, Beatrice thought the planet had a welcoming glow about it. "Hey, isn't that where—"

"My home!" exclaimed Samma.

Padinny and Keena came over to look. Keena joked, "If you look close enough, you can see Samma's mom. Hi, Mom!" Padinny and Keena giggled.

Samma laughed and then sighed.

"Do you miss it?" asked Beatrice.

"Very much," said Samma. "I miss my family and friends. I miss my school and my bedroom. It's hard to be away from them for so long. I know that time doesn't pass on our missions, but I still miss them."

"Yeah," said Beatrice with a sympathetic look in her eyes. "I mean, I even miss my younger brother!" she added as a joke.

Samma laughed. "The truth is I have a new family here, as part of the POGs."

"Yeah, but can they make you Galla?" asked Graniten as he handed Samma a glass of the sweet liquid.

"Ha! You wish!" said Samma as she took a sip. "Galla is my mother's special recipe. No one knows the secret ingredient. All she told me was that it is found somewhere on Venus."

Keena thought for a second. "Hmm, Venus, right? Maybe the secret ingredient is *gas*!" and Keena made a fart sound with his mouth. Everyone laughed, and Samma playfully punched Keena on the shoulder.

Rala came over and said, "Oh Keena, Keena, Keena, you are such a comedian! Just remember, when we get to Mercury you're on my turf, so you better watch out!"

"Ooh, I'm shaking," joked Keena, and he shot a fireball across the room.

Rala calmly held up her hands and grabbed the fireball out of the air. Then she moved her hands around it, and poof – turned it into a ball!

"What?!" exclaimed Beatrice as Rala threw the ball at Keena, who caught it and started running around the ship. "Hey! Come back here!" shouted Rala.

"Guys!" yelled Samma, "What have I said? No POG ball on the ship. Wait until we land."

"Yes, Mom," both Keena and Rala said, laughing.

"That is amazing!" said Beatrice.

Rala smiled and looked out the window. "If you think

that's amazing, look out your window."

Beatrice turned, and there in front of her was Mercury. She pressed her face against the window and stared intently at the fiery, orange planet below. It was like nothing she had seen before or even dreamed about. It was beautiful. Flames burst out of every corner. The colors were magical – red, purple, orange, and even blue shades across the planet.

Just then, Samma snapped her head back and yelled out, "Attention! All POGs on deck. You know the drill. Graniten, punch in the landing coordinates for 100 meters south of SEAK. Padinny, velocity update. Let's keep it under 1000 mph upon entry to make it as smooth as possible. Jana …."

Beatrice watched in dizzying amazement as the ship sprang to life. The joking and the laughing were replaced with intense concentration. All of a sudden, the POGs were very disciplined and focused.

"Okay," said Samma sitting back down in the large captain's chair. "Let's land this ship!"

Beatrice felt a light tap on her shoulder. "You may want to buckle up," came Padinny's soft voice as she sat in the seat next to Beatrice.

"Thanks," Beatrice said as she sat down and buckled her seatbelt. Beatrice sat and watched as the ship got closer to Mercury.

"Thrusters on, Cannie!" barked Samma.

Cannie pushed a giant red button, and the thrusters started with a huge bang that startled Beatrice. She let out a yelp.

Once again Padinny said, "Don't worry, Beatrice. We've

done this hundreds of times. It's fun!"

Just then, the spaceship shot forward, then dipped down with its nose facing Mercury. Beatrice's eyes grew wide in fear. They were actually facing straight down!

The ship sprang ahead, forcing Beatrice to fall back hard in her seat. Down they went, bursting into Mercury's atmosphere and emerging onto a new planet. The ship continued to speed ahead, getting closer and closer to the ground.

"Jana, please engage rear-propulsion engine!" shouted Samma.

Jana hit a few buttons on the wall, and in a split instant, the entire ship flipped around so the nose was pointed straight up in the air! The rear thrusters then came on and gradually lowered the ship more and more slowly until it landed with a slight thud on the ground.

"Wahoo!" yelled Keena.

"That was fun!" grinned Graniten.

Samma smiled as the engine powered down. "Great work everyone. Don't forget your masks."

"Masks?" asked Beatrice.

Samma looked over at Beatrice and laughed. "Oh, right! I knew I forgot something. Since we are all from different planets with different atmospheres and different temperatures, we cannot walk on other planets without getting hurt."

"Oh," said Beatrice with a quizzical look.

"But don't worry!" replied Samma. "Years ago, an alien from Jupiter invented a mask that regulates atmospheric gas and body temperature so that we can be on any planet at any time."

"Wow," said Beatrice. "Any relation to Padinny?"

Samma gave a deep sigh while gathering up some items next to the captain's chair and putting them into her backpack. "More on that later, Beatrice. For now, we must get to Jobu and test your locket."

"Okay, sounds good," said Beatrice, a little confused. "Why didn't Samma want to tell me about this alien?" she thought to herself. "Who was he?"

Before she could think further, there was a light tap on her elbow. It was Padinny, holding a bright blue mask.

"This is for you," said Padinny in a quiet voice.

"Thanks," said Beatrice, grabbing hold of the mask. "Does it work like a SCUBA mask?"

Padinny looked up at Beatrice with a confused look. "What's SCUBA?"

"Oh!" replied Beatrice. "SCUBA is a device we use on Earth to breathe underwater."

Padinny giggled. "You mean you can't breathe underwater?"

Beatrice's eyes got wide. "Umm, no, can you?"

Padinny glanced into Beatrice's eyes with a serious look, then, all of a sudden, burst into laughter. "Of course not, silly! No one can breathe underwater!"

Beatrice laughed. She liked Padinny a lot.

Padinny gestured to Beatrice. "Lean down. I'll get it on you and show you how it works."

Beatrice got on her knees so Padinny could reach her head. Padinny slipped the mask strap over Beatrice's head and attached an X-shaped electronic device on her chest. She then connected a cord from the mask to the X. The X immediately began to emit a blue light.

Padinny moved a dial on the X over to the left and hit a green button. "All set!" she said. "You are now able to be on Mercury!"

"Thanks, Padinny," said Beatrice with a smile.

Beatrice walked down the long, white hallway of the spaceship toward the back door. Graniten pulled a long lever, the door swung open, and one by one, the POGs exited the spaceship. When it was Beatrice's turn, she stopped at the door, took a deep breath, and stepped out onto Mercury's surface.

It was amazing! Beatrice just stood there and couldn't believe her eyes. It was so bright! There were fires everywhere, but not the kind of fires she knew of on Earth. These fires were more beautiful than scary, almost like giant rainbows made of flames. The ground was mostly dirt and rock.

Rala came over and put her arm around Beatrice and took a satisfied breath. "Welcome to my home! Pretty awesome, isn't it?"

"Yes," replied Beatrice, still staring ahead at the sun, which was very, very close compared to its distance to Earth. "Is it safe for us to be here?"

Samma walked up beside Beatrice. "Of course it is. Thanks to information gathered by other POGs over the years, we know precisely how long we can stay on each planet, and how to protect ourselves from unique atmospheric elements. Don't worry, Beatrice, we've done this before. Enjoy!"

Beatrice smiled. "I'll try," she said as she walked ahead with the group. Up ahead she saw a small, red building surrounded by orange and white flames.

"Wow," said Beatrice, "what's that?"

"That," responded a very excited Rala, "is SEAK!" As Rala spoke, the POGs all started running toward the small building. They were laughing and yelling in excitement. Beatrice ran after them, not sure what to expect.

When they arrived at the front gate, a bellowing voice

stopped them in their tracks. "HALT!"

Everyone froze. Beatrice looked around her and saw fear on the faces of the POGs.

"Who goes there?" came the voice again.

Beatrice's eyes widened, and she felt very scared. Maybe something happened at SEAK? Maybe Jobu had been captured by the Bracas? Should she run? Could her locket help? Before she could think further, Graniten snickered, Jana giggled, and everyone around her began to laugh.

Beatrice looked ahead in confusion.

"Oh, Jobu," said Keena leaning down and slapping the ground as he laughed hysterically, "you got the newbie good!"

"Good one!" shouted Cannie. "You should have seen the look on her face!"

Beatrice had no clue what was going on. Then she saw an alien walk toward the front gate. She was a small alien with enormous eyes – many eyes. So many, in fact, that Beatrice couldn't count them all. She had two long antennae, two short legs, and four arms!

Samma put her arm around Beatrice. "Beatrice, meet Jobu. Jobu, this is Beatrice, the POG from Earth."

Jobu pushed a button next to the gate, and the fiery outline disappeared. She walked out slowly, and all four of her arms reached out to grab Beatrice's hand. In a slow, calm voice she said, "Beatrice, it is an honor to meet you. I know this has been quite the day for you, but please trust that you are in good hands here."

"Yeah, four hands!" joked Keena. Everyone laughed.

Jobu smiled. "We will take great care of you and keep

you safe!"

She then turned to everyone else and said, "Hello, my precious POGs. Come and give Jobu a hug!"

The POGs erupted in cheers and ran up to hug Jobu. Everyone was smiling.

"Welcome back!" announced Jobu. "I know these have been difficult times, but I believe that you have brought good news with you." She gestured to Beatrice. "Time is of the essence. Let's get inside and test Beatrice's locket to see if it truly provides us with accurate coordinates to the remaining power buckets."

At that, she turned and walked back through the front gate toward the entrance to SEAK. The other POGs, all smiling, followed close behind, talking and laughing. They seemed so happy to be back at SEAK.

Beatrice followed past the front gate and ducked her head under the small doorway that led into SEAK. Unlike the cardboard spaceship that changed into a huge spaceship when she entered, SEAK was actually small, yet cozy. There were many small rooms down long hallways with very low ceilings. There was a smell that Beatrice couldn't place. Was it lavender? Some kind of flower? She couldn't tell what it was, but somehow it reminded her of home. Beatrice roamed aimlessly for a while, taking it all in. She found a wall down one hallway that was covered with all kinds of pictures of different aliens. One was of the current POGs all standing together, smiling.

"Wow!" exclaimed Beatrice.

"Pretty awesome, huh?" said Keena, appearing next to Beatrice in the hallway. "SEAK is quite the special place, full of so many great memories of being here and learning from Jobu!" Keena then took his mask off.

"Wait!" cried Beatrice.

"Oh, don't worry," reassured Kenna. "Jobu has set the atmosphere inside SEAK to the same setting of the spaceship, so everyone can walk around without masks. Go ahead, take yours off. I promise it's safe."

As Beatrice took her mask off, she saw Samma down the hall in a tense conversation with Jobu. Samma looked a little frustrated. She gestured fast with her yellow hands until Jobu waved her off and turned to walk back to where the POGs had gathered. "What could they be talking about?" Beatrice wondered to herself.

"Follow me, POGs," said Jobu as they walked down the hallway and into a larger room with a long white table, green chairs, and giant black screen on the wall.

Jobu gestured for everyone to sit. "Everyone," she began, "let's get to it. Padinny, please project an image of the galaxy."

Padinny hit a few buttons on her POG-Watch and projected an image of the galaxy onto the black screen.

Beatrice," continued Jobu in a calm, methodical voice, "please open your locket and direct the light onto the screen."

As Beatrice walked to the front of the room, she felt nervous and excited all at once. *What if it didn't work? What if it did?* She also had a random thought about her new bicycle. When would she get to ride it? She hoped her brother hadn't knocked it over. *Wait, time hadn't passed, so he couldn't have touched her bicycle!* Beatrice's head felt a little jumbled.

She was interrupted by Jobu saying, "Whenever you're

ready, Beatrice."

Beatrice stood there quietly, reached down, and slowly opened the locket. Light poured out of the locket, and just as it had done on the ship, the light hit different parts of the projected map. At the top of the screen were the words MAP OF POWER BUCKETS.

"Amazing," said Jobu, looking intently at the beams of light on the map. "Padinny, please enter the exact coordinates for SEAK." Padinny punched in some numbers, and the map zoomed in to an overhead image of SEAK. There, just a bit to the right of the school, was a beam of light.

"There!" shouted Kenna.

"Yes!" exclaimed Cannie.

Jobu smiled and turned to face everyone. "Padinny, please store those coordinates, and let's set up an exploratory mission to the location to see if power buckets are present. It shouldn't be far from here, but we will want to be safe."

"Yes, Jobu!" said everyone together as they stood up to leave the room.

"Beatrice, a moment," said Jobu. Beatrice turned in surprise, and saw Samma standing in the doorway with a pleading look in her eyes. Jobu gestured her away with four hands and said, "Please sit, my dear. We need to talk."

Jobu

Beatrice sat down and nervously fidgeted in her chair. What was this all about?

"Beatrice," began Jobu as she closed the door and began to pace back and forth, "there is a lot you don't know about POGs, our history, and how we got here. What I'm about to tell you may surprise you, but please know that it is all real, all true." Jobu paused for a bit, then went on. "Samma wants to protect you from the truth and believes that you are not yet ready to hear the full story."

Jobu kept pacing. "I understand her point of view and know that she cares about you. However, I believe that if you are to truly help us against the Bracas, you need to understand where we all come from."

"Come from?" asked a bewildered Beatrice.

Jobu continued without addressing Beatrice. "Many, many years ago, I helped form the POGs after the Great Battle, which was an intergalactic war fought between planets for control of the galaxy. The Great Battle devastated many planets, hurt many aliens, and displaced millions of aliens from their home planets." Jobu sighed, "Such a sad time for the whole galaxy."

"That sounds terrible," said Beatrice. "Why were so many aliens forced from their home planets?"

Jobu sighed again. "They were fleeing for their lives. You see, the Great Battle was started by an evil yet powerful alien from Pluto named Torbodox."

"Pluto?" said Beatrice, "But I thought Pluto

wasn't a planet?"

"It isn't anymore," replied Jobu. "But once upon a time it was a magnificent place. After the Great Battle, Pluto was so unstable it had to be taken off the list of inhabitable planets."

"So, this Torbodox," said Beatrice, "what did he do?"

"Torbodox wanted one thing: to control the galaxy by being the most powerful alien. He spent years going from planet to planet, building an army of like-minded supporters. Torbodox and his army didn't like that aliens were free to travel from planet to planet. They didn't like that aliens from Jupiter could live on Mars or that aliens from Mercury could have a family on Neptune. These aliens were angry, and when Torbodox gave the order, they started wars on each planet at the exact same time."

Jobu turned to look at Beatrice. "Everyone was caught by surprise. As a result of each planet being under attack, no planet could help another planet. It was complete chaos. The planetary wars continued, and many lives were lost on each side. At the same time, Torbodox and his army released a special gas on each planet that changed the unique atmosphere, making each planet uninhabitable. All aliens were forced to leave their planets and live in spaceships in outer space."

"Wait," said Beatrice, "you said the planets were uninhabitable, but aliens live on them now. What changed?"

"Great observation, my dear," said Jobu. "Torbodox was finally captured, and his army defeated. Then it was time to rebuild the galaxy. It was a dark time," said Jobu, a sad glint in her eyes. "You see, all aliens were living in spaceships throughout outer space. In order to support and maintain all these spaceships, power buckets were in high demand. I don't know how much you know about power buckets, but they are very special."

Beatrice interjected, "Keena told me they are like a kind of fuel. They are how you move around the galaxy."

"Precisely," said Jobu. "Without power buckets, we would be stuck on a planet with no chance to move anywhere. Since aliens had to remain in space, they needed to use a great number of power buckets to fly around."

Jobu's four hands gestured in the air. "It was at this time that I met Scarab, a brilliant alien from Jupiter. Scarab was working on reversing the effects of the gas Torbodox had released. We set up a lab and, after years and years of trying, were finally able to stabilize the atmospheres on each planet. Unfortunately, this meant that only aliens born on Mercury could live on Mercury or aliens born on Jupiter could live on Jupiter. While this helped many of the aliens to return home, many more were still left wandering in outer space. We needed something that would allow all aliens to live and travel anywhere in the galaxy just like before the Great Battle."

Jobu furrowed her brow and closed many of her eyes. "Around this time, power buckets began getting stolen. Aliens relied on them a great deal, and bands of vandals popped up around the galaxy, each trying to steal the power buckets to either keep or sell to the highest bidder. It was ugly. Finally, Scarab managed to perfect his mask, and we had the upper hand! Together, Scarab and I gathered together more aliens, one from each planet, and we tasked ourselves with protecting the power buckets from the thieves and vandals. We spent years mapping the locations of power buckets on the different planets. We stored the information inside eight lockets, and each POG received a locket that contained the coordinates to the power buckets. Then things began to unravel."

Jobu stared intently at Beatrice.

"Scarab went bad. He formed a group called the Bracas, and they started to steal power buckets. We didn't know what to do since Scarab was the most powerful POG with one of the lockets!"

"But why would Scarab and the Bracas need or even want all the power buckets?" asked Beatrice.

Jobu looked forlorn. "Because they wanted the same thing Torbodox wanted: to control the galaxy. Scarab saw that if he controlled the power buckets, then he could control the movement of all aliens in the galaxy. Without power buckets, aliens would be unable to move from planet to planet. He would be the leader of the galaxy."

"But you and the other POGs each have lockets. Couldn't you just gather the power buckets?" asked Beatrice.

Jobu held up her hands. "We *had* the lockets. With the help of the Bracas, Scarab turned his attention to us, the other POGs. He knew that if he wanted to control the galaxy he would need all eight lockets. One by one he managed to fight and defeat the other POGs and steal their lockets, thus gaining access to the location of the power buckets. He even came after me. After a very long battle, he managed to steal my locket, but I managed to escape and make my way here to Mercury, where I set up a protected school called SEAK. It became my mission to teach other POGs so they can protect the galaxy from the likes of Scarab and the Bracas. I have taught many POGs over the years, but tonight is the first time I have seen one of the original lockets in a very, very long time."

Beatrice sat there, silent, not sure what to say. She had so many questions and didn't know where to begin. "I guess I'm a little confused."

"How so, my dear?" said Jobu.

"If Scarab defeated all the POGs and stole all the lockets, then how did I get this?" and Beatrice gently touched the orange locket hanging around her neck.

Jobu smiled and took Beatrice's hand. "Well, luckily Scarab didn't get all eight lockets. One POG managed to escape with a locket and disappear without a trace. That is until today, your tenth birthday."

Beatrice stared ahead looking very puzzled. "What does my birthday have to do with this?"

"Beatrice," said Jobu with a calm and steady voice, "the POG who escaped with the locket was your father."

eatrice tried to speak, but no sound came out. She just sat there staring at the wall. Her dad? How could he be a POG? He was just...well, he was just a dad! From Earth!

Then she remembered his wink after giving her the locket.

"Maybe you can put it in your spaceship to remind you of home when you are flying in space."

Beatrice had thought he was kidding, being his normal goofball self, talking about space. Wait, *space*? Beatrice's dad was always telling her stories about space aliens and a great battle.

"Oh, my, gosh," Beatrice thought to herself. "Could my dad really be a POG?!"

She had assumed that the orange locket had come from a store. But what had he said after he gave her the locket?

"That locket has been in our family for many years and is very special. Take great care of it. It may look like a normal locket, but it's been known to help in times of need."

Beatrice had thought he was kidding...about everything! He was always joking. But after everything that had happened, it all started to make a bit of sense. Beatrice's dad knew what was going on. He knew she'd find out about the POGs. He knew she'd fly to space. He knew about Jobu. He knew everything!

As Beatrice sat there staring at the wall, working through things in her head, Jobu sat quietly, patiently, letting Beatrice come to terms with everything on her own.

"Jobu," Beatrice finally managed to say out loud. "If what you say about my dad is true, it still doesn't explain how you knew to find me today. How did you know that I would build the spaceship? How did you know that I would have the locket?"

Jobu smiled. "These are all excellent questions, Beatrice. Let's just say we had some help from an old friend."

Beatrice looked confused. "Who?" she asked.

"Your father, my dear, your father."

"But how? We live on Earth, and you said that the POG who escaped actually disappeared without a trace. If he truly escaped Scarab and the Bracas, then how did he contact you? Wouldn't that put him in danger?"

Jobu waited patiently and then said, "When it became clear that Scarab was defeating the POGs and stealing all the lockets, your father and I devised a dangerous yet necessary plan. As the last two remaining POGs, we decided that I would stay and fight Scarab and your father would leave and hide."

"Why?" asked Beatrice.

"As long as one POG remained hidden, it would make it impossible for Scarab to control all the lockets in the galaxy. This was a very difficult decision, and your father was not happy about leaving me behind.

"So, he didn't know you survived your battle

against Scarab?"

"No," said Jobu, staring off. "Not for a long while. Scarab and I had a long and hard fight." Jobu looked off into the distance. "He is such a powerful alien, capable of immense destruction, but," Jobu added with a smile, "I'm pretty good myself!"

Beatrice smiled, and Jobu continued with the story. "After the battle, Scarab retreated to Jupiter with the remaining Bracas along with seven of the eight lockets. I was injured pretty badly, but I survived and made my way here to Mercury. After I recovered, I discovered that I did not have the strength to fight anymore. My powers were still great, but my body was slower and weaker than before. As a result, I built SEAK and dedicated my life to training other aliens to fight the Bracas and work to get the lockets back."

"Wow," said Beatrice. "That must have been a very scary time."

"It was a period of great uncertainty in the galaxy. Aliens were nervous. But I had a new mission, and I worked tirelessly to identify and train new generations of POGs."

So, this whole time you didn't know where my father was or even if Scarab had gotten the last locket?"

"That's right," replied Jobu. "I carefully monitored activities in the galaxy, and over the years I eventually learned enough to know that Scarab was still searching for the last locket. This meant that your father had survived!"

"That's amazing!" said Beatrice. "But how did you contact him?"

Jobu smiled and gestured to Beatrice's wrist watch.

"Nice watch," she said.

"Thanks," said a confused Beatrice.

"Where did you get it?"

"Oh, well, Rala formed it out of light for me. She wanted me to have a POG-Watch like the other POGs."

"That was very nice of her," said Jobu. "Do you know what it does?"

"Umm," stuttered Beatrice. "lots of things?"

Jobu laughed. "Yes, it is a versatile tool that allows the POGs to have access to a computer at all times. I developed these watches along with Scarab many years ago. The original ones were much bigger and much slower. Ah, technology!"

Beatrice looked down at her watch. "I still don't understand."

"When I realized that Scarab was still looking for your father's locket, I also realized that Scarab's POG-Watch must have been destroyed. You see, my dear, each POG-Watch also serves as a satellite and communication device between POGs! It tells us where each POG is located at any time. Isn't that awesome?" Jobu smiled brightly.

"You mean, like a smartphone?" said a puzzled Beatrice.

"A what?"

"A smartphone," continued Beatrice. "We have them all over Earth. You can send messages to anyone on the planet instantaneously. It's pretty cool. You can even send pictures and post them online. Seriously, everyone has them…."

Jobu's eyes became big, and she stared at Beatrice.

"You Earthlings and your technology!" and Jobu laughed. "Since I knew that Scarab couldn't contact us or determine our location, I held out hope that your father still had his POG-Watch. I sent a message out into space every single day for more than ten years."

"Wow!" said Beatrice. "And you didn't hear anything?"

"No, not until one month ago. I got a very short response that simply gave a date, September 29th, 2018, along with the coordinates for your house."

"My birthday? Coordinates for my house?" asked an incredulous Beatrice.

"Precisely," replied Jobu. "I wasn't sure if it was a trap or not, but I had faith in your father, so I sent the POGs to investigate. It appears as if I was right to trust him!"

Beatrice looked at her locket. "He planned the whole thing. He sent you the date and location, and he made sure that I made a ship and had the locket. He was preparing me this whole time!"

"He always was very smart," smiled Jobu with a nostalgic smile on her face.

Beatrice thought for a moment and then said, "But I thought Samma said that the POGs were attacked by the Bracas on their way to Earth and that they crash landed. That's why they needed my ship."

Jobu sighed. "Sadly, that's true. It seems the Bracas were out patrolling around Venus tonight. They spotted the POGs and chased them all around Venus until the Bracas managed to strike the POGs with an ice missile, causing the POGs to crash into Earth's atmosphere."

"Wow," said Beatrice. "Why didn't the Bracas pursue the POGs to Earth?"

Jobu raised all of her many eyebrows. "That, my dear, is a question for which I have no answer. It was a blessing in disguise. The POGs managed to make it to the coordinates – your house – and that's when Samma found you."

Beatrice sat there in silence, glancing at the yellow wall of the room. She looked down the long hallway and spotted Padinny and Samma walking together pushing buttons on a small computer. Keena and Cannie were goofing around in the distance, laughing.

"Who exactly is Scarab?" Beatrice asked.

Jobu turned quickly as Padinny walked into the room. "Er, um, that is a discussion for a different day. We've already talked about so much. Let's change gears and talk about the mission! Padinny, any updates?"

Padinny smiled, sat down next to Jobu, and began to discuss the plan to test the locket's coordinates.

Beatrice sat with a thoughtful look on her face. Why didn't Jobu want to talk about Scarab? Why did she get so flustered when Padinny walked in the room? Was there a connection between Padinny and Scarab? So many questions! Beatrice was growing frustrated at having more questions than answers, but she figured the only way to get answers was to go along with the plan and search for the power buckets.

Samma, Keena, and Cannie entered the room, closed the door, and sat down at the long silver table. Jobu gestured to Padinny, "The floor is yours!"

P adinny stood up and slowly but confidently hit some white buttons on her POG-Watch. Immediately a map of the area around SEAK displayed on the wall. Padinny had circled one of the power bucket locations.

"Okay, everybody," she began in a quiet yet even voice, "you have been selected as part of the exploratory team to check on the coordinates for the power buckets."

"Cool!" interrupted Keena. "Maybe Cannie and I will get to blast some Bracas!" Cannie and Keena high-fived each other to the dismay of Samma and Jobu.

"Please," said Jobu, "the purpose of this mission is to test Beatrice's locket and see if it provides accurate coordinates to the power buckets. We do not want to fight any Bracas. However, in case the Bracas are nearby, you two are being brought along to provide protection."

"Okay, Jobu, we understand," said Keena, winking over at Cannie, who gave a smile.

"Please continue, Padinny," said Jobu.

Padinny went on, "Beatrice please open your locket."

Beatrice nodded and opened the locket, directing a stream of light onto Padinny's map.

Padinny continued. "We will establish a perimeter around the power buckets here," and she pointed to the circled area. "After a perimeter is set, we will send Beatrice and Samma in closer to collect them. Once our mission is complete, we will fall back and head straight back to SEAK. This is to be a quick and focused mission. No dilly-dallying and no joking around, please," she added glancing over at Keena and Cannie. "Any questions?"

Beatrice, feeling a little confused, slowly raised her hand. All eyes turned to her.

"Yes, Beatrice," said Padinny.

"What do we do with the power buckets once we find them?"

Padinny smiled, "Of course! How could I forget to go over that with you, Beatrice? Power buckets can only be picked up by these special gloves my father designed back on Jupiter." Padinny held up a pair of the gloves and threw them over to Samma, who caught them and put them on. The gloves were red and black and resembled snow gloves Beatrice had worn the previous winter during a huge blizzard.

Samma said, "Once we find the power buckets I will pick them up and put them in my backpack."

"Okay," replied Beatrice, only somewhat less confused.

Padinny saw the look on Beatrice's face. "Don't worry, Beatrice," she said. "You just need to get us to the power buckets. Once there, let us take care of the rest."

Beatrice thought for a second. "What do you need me for? Can't you just use this map and go find them on your own?"

Samma interjected, "I wish it were that simple, Beatrice. I really do. However, remember that power buckets are constantly moving. Your locket provides exact coordinates for power buckets at any given time. This is a huge advantage for us to stay one step ahead of Scarab and the Bracas."

"Wow," said Beatrice, "this locket is pretty special."

Beatrice stopped and thought for a moment. "You know, I've been thinking and wondering who made the lockets in the first place?"

Samma sighed, and Padinny furrowed her brow. Keena and Cannie looked down at the ground. It was Jobu who finally spoke, "That's not important right now. Let's just prepare for the mission. Please be careful, everybody."

"We will!" everyone piped in together.

Samma, Beatrice, Keena, Cannie, and Padinny walked out of the room and down the hall to a large room that resembled a mechanic's garage. There were machines everywhere with all kinds of computers blinking and beeping. Graniten, Rala, and Jana were all busy working but stopped what they were doing when the other POGs entered. Rala gave a wave to Beatrice as she walked by. Beatrice waved back, feeling a bit nervous. The other aliens put on their masks, so Beatrice did the same.

Samma turned to face everyone. "Okay, listen up. We have a general location, so follow my lead. Once we get closer, we will use Beatrice's locket to find the exact coordinates of the power buckets, gather them up, and bring them straight back to SEAK. This is an exploratory mission, so remember to keep a tight formation. Cannie and Keena, you are our eyes. Stay alert. Graniten, Rala, and Jana, you will serve as backup for this mission. Keep the spaceship on standby and be ready to come lend us support if we run into any trouble.

"Not a problem!" said Jana with a serious look in her eyes. All of a sudden, her eyes turned dark blue, and she shot ice out of them into the air.

"Wow!" yelled Beatrice.

Jana smiled and looked over at Beatrice with dark blue eyes. "I'll be watching you!"

Beatrice gulped. She was feeling a bit more nervous than before.

"Everyone ready?"

"Yes, Samma!" shouted everyone except Beatrice.

Cannie pulled a large grey lever at the back of the garage, and a huge door opened. One by one, the POGs walked out onto the hot, rocky ground of Mercury.

"Keep a steady formation, Cannie!" yelled Samma. "Keena, remember you are on lookout."

Padinny walked ahead, staring down at the map on her POG-Watch. As they walked, Beatrice looked around her, taking in Mercury's beautiful terrain. There were flames bursting from rocks, bright lights flashing across the atmosphere from the all-too-close sun, and bubbly lava. It was like nothing Beatrice had ever seen or even read about in a book. It was absolutely magnificent.

She must have stopped walking because all of a sudden, a voice said, "Earth to Beatrice?" Beatrice turned to see a laughing Cannie. "Get it? 'Earth to Beatrice?' Because you're from Earth!"

"Good one, Cannie!" yelled Keena from the front of the line.

Samma sighed. Beatrice smiled. Keena and Cannie helped her relax a bit.

The POGs kept walking a while longer until Padinny held up her hand. "Team, we are in the general area of the power buckets. It's time to use Beatrice's locket to find exact coordinates."

Padinny hit a button on her watch, and a map of the area appeared as a hologram in front of them.

"Whenever you're ready, Beatrice."

Beatrice took a deep breath and grabbed her locket. She didn't know why she was so nervous. She thought that maybe her new friends wouldn't like her anymore if the locket didn't work. But she had to try.

She smiled, took a deep breath, and twisted open her locket. Light streamed out, and she directed it onto the hologram map of the area. Padinny hit some buttons, and one particular area lit up in bright, flashing orange.

"There!" exclaimed Padinny. She immediately typed something into her POG-Watch and said, "Follow me!" The aliens raced over a ridge covered in fire until they reached a very large brown and grey boulder.

Padinny stopped and so did everyone else. "According to the locket, the power buckets should be here."

"Right here?" asked Cannie.

"I don't see anything," offered Keena as he walked around the boulder.

"Me either," said Cannie, tapping the boulder with his arm.

"Maybe the power buckets are inside," offered Padinny.

Keena frowned. "Inside? How can we get the power buckets if they are inside a gigantic boulder covered in fire?"

Samma thought for a moment. "What would Jobu tell us to do? She would say to work as a team. Use our collective powers. Let's see if I can give us a clearer image of what's inside." She stood up and walked to the front of the boulder. As she held up her hands, her palms began to glow brighter and brighter. Thousands of beams of light began moving around until they formed a clear image of the inside of the boulder. There, in the corner of the boulder, sat a pile of beautiful golden rings. Power buckets!

"I see the power buckets!" shouted Keena as he raced toward them. All of a sudden, *THWACK!* Keena smashed into the boulder.

"Ouch!" he yelled, falling back onto the ground.

"Are you okay?" laughed Cannie as he went over to help. "That was pretty silly, Keena!"

"Yeah, I guess," giggled Keena as he rubbed his head. "What happened?"

"Hmm," said Samma. "It appears that I was able to give us a glimpse inside the boulder, but the outside of the boulder still remains. We are going to have to try other powers to figure out how to get inside."

"Sounds good to me!" shouted an excited Cannie. He walked up and shot ice missiles at the boulder, but they melted before hitting. "Rats!" he said.

"My turn," said Padinny, as she slowly walked to the front. She gently touched the X's on her chest with her hands and immediately produced beautiful bolts of lightning.

"Wow!" said Beatrice as she looked at the beams of electricity shooting out of Padinny's chest. Unfortunately, the lightning bolts fizzled in the gaseous atmosphere of Mercury.

"Anyone else?" asked Padinny.

All of a sudden, Beatrice felt herself being pulled toward the boulder. Her locket was glowing brighter and brighter.

"My turn," said Keena, and he shot a huge fireball at the boulder. However, the fire just bounced off the already-burning boulder.

"Umm, guys," Beatrice said, somewhat nervously. No one noticed. "Hey, a little help here," she called out as she was being pulled closer to the boulder. Finally, as she reached the boulder, she yelled out, *"Help!"*

Before any of the other POGs could react, Beatrice reached the sharp edge of the boulder, moved through, and landed with a thud right next to the glowing pile of power buckets. She sat there, staring at the power buckets, amazed at how bright they were, unable to figure out how she had ended up inside the boulder.

Silence. The POGs were speechless.

Keena gasped. "What?! How is she—?"

"Um, I don't know about you guys, but that that was way cool," interrupted Cannie.

Samma stared in amazement. "That is one special locket!"

Padinny, ever focused on the task at hand, said, "Beatrice, in addition to your locket providing us with coordinates to the power buckets, it seems it also acts as a gravitational force to draw you to them."

"Okay," muttered a stunned Beatrice.

Padinny went on. "This is amazing! We need you to

come back out and put on the gloves."

Samma pulled the gloves out of her backpack and said, "You have to wear these gloves to pick up the power buckets; otherwise they can greatly injure you."

"I'll try," said an astonished Beatrice. She turned her body and grabbed hold of the locket. Nothing happened.

"Come on, Beatrice," said Padinny. "You can do it!"

Beatrice tried again. Her locket remained dark. "No, I can't!" said Beatrice, struggling to move inside the boulder. "I—I can't move."

"What do you mean?" asked Samma.

"While you were trying to get inside the boulder, I could feel something drag me closer and closer. There was a force that wanted to bring me inside the boulder. I didn't try! It just happened!"

"How could that be?" asked Samma.

Cannie and Keena looked confused.

Padinny was busy hitting buttons on her POG-Watch and looking lost in thought.

Beatrice turned her head to look at her alien friends. "Hey guys, why don't I just pick them up and carry them out? They aren't that big."

Padinny's head shot up as she yelled, "*No!!* Do not do that. The power buckets are too dangerous!"

As Padinny was talking, Beatrice's locket began to glow again. "Hey look!" shouted Cannie, "the locket is alive!"

Beatrice looked down to see the locket glowing brighter and brighter and feeling warmer and warmer until it sprang open and out shot a direct beam of white light that led to the power buckets.

"Are you okay, Beatrice?" yelled out Samma.

"I think so," said Beatrice. "It's pretty strange. I'm not controlling this at all."

As the POGs looked on in amazement, the power buckets lifted off the ground and, carried by the light, floated over to Beatrice. In an instant, the power buckets flew inside her locket, the light went out, and Beatrice was thrown out of the boulder, landing on the ground with a giant *THUD*.

"Are you all right?" asked Keena, offering his hand to help Beatrice up.

"Um, I think so," replied a dazed Beatrice, brushing herself off.

Everyone stared in amazement.

"That was incredible," Cannie said with all four eyes wide.

"How ...?" trailed off Samma walking over and putting her arm around Beatrice.

Padinny stood across from Beatrice and Samma, staring into space.

"Padinny, please say something," said Samma. "What do you think happened?"

But Padinny couldn't speak. Her face was frozen in fear, looking past Beatrice and Samma into the distance.

"What is it, Padinny?" asked Samma, suddenly more alert.

Padinny just stared ahead, fear in her eyes, and finally pointed up behind Samma and Beatrice. The POGs all turned at once, in time to see a dark figure floating down from the sky above.

Scarab

Beatrice stared hard at the figure, examining his large purple body, bright red helmet, long brown cape, and dark red gloves and boots. The gloves reminded Beatrice of the gloves Padinny had given Samma to use to grab the power buckets. He was immensely tall and towered over the POGs as he hovered in the air above them. Beatrice couldn't be sure, but she thought she saw a locket around his neck. Behind him flew four similarly dressed large and strong-looking aliens with menacing looks. Seconds felt like hours.

"What is going on?" Beatrice thought to herself. She looked over at the other POGs to see them all alert and ready to fight.

It was Keena who finally broke the silence. "Scarab, what are you doing here?"

Beatrice's eyes got as big as grapefruits. "Scarab!" she thought, panic filling her body. "How did he know they would be here?!" Fear welled up inside her.

"Hello, POGs," Scarab said in a steady, deep voice. "What a coincidence to find you here."

Samma stepped up in front of Beatrice, shielding her from Scarab, and said in a bold voice, "We aren't looking for trouble, Scarab. You and your crew of Bracas should turn around and leave now!"

Scarab looked down at Samma, rolled his eyes, and peered over her shoulder at Beatrice. "What do we have here?" he said in a sneaky, slithering voice. "A new POG?"

"Leave her out of this, Scarab," demanded Samma.

"Hmm," began Scarab, still floating above the POGs, "you must be the POG from Earth. What is your name, child?"

Beatrice couldn't speak. Fear had completely gripped her body, and her tongue was too weak to move.

"You look familiar," continued Scarab. "Do I know you from somewhere?" A wry smile appeared on his face.

Beatrice looked around her. The other POGs stood firm, looking confident and brave. But Padinny stood alone, with her head down, unable to face Scarab. Beatrice thought about how helpful and kind Padinny had been to her. She owed it to Padinny to be brave.

She stepped to the side of Samma, puffed out her chest, and in a strong voice said, "I don't believe we've met, but I know all about you, Scarab."

"She speaks!" exclaimed Scarab, and the other Bracas laughed. "You know all about me, huh? Well, *Beatrice*, I know all about you!"

Beatrice froze. *How could Scarab know about her? Who had told him?*

Confusion must have shown on Beatrice's face. Scarab laughed. "Oh, sweet, naive Beatrice. Hasn't Jobu told you anything?"

Beatrice looked up into Scarab's red eyes and gave him a defiant look. "Jobu told me enough!"

"Oh really? I find that hard to believe."

"She told me how you turned evil and stole lockets from the other POGs in an attempt to control the galaxy!"

Scarab began to laugh, slowly at first, and then faster

and faster, louder and louder. "Jobu would say that! I mean, did she tell you the real story? Did she tell you that your father and I were once best friends?"

Beatrice looked shocked.

Scarab went on. "Oh, you didn't know that, did you? Did she tell you that your father and I worked together for years, helping millions of aliens live freer and better lives?"

Beatrice looked down at her shoes. "You expect me to believe that?"

Scarab flew down and landed gently on the ground, no more than 10 meters from where Beatrice and Samma were standing. The other Bracas stayed in the air. The POGs held their positions and looked ready to fight.

Scarab's voice softened a little. "Yes, my dear, your father and I were best friends." Scarab looked up at the sky. Then he looked back down, and his menacing look had returned. "We *were* best friends until your father turned on me! He tried to prevent me from creating something truly wonderful in the galaxy."

Samma interjected. "You mean stealing all the power buckets so you can be the supreme ruler of the galaxy?"

Beatrice looked over at Samma. Samma was red in the face and breathing hard. She looked fierce and seemed not at all afraid of Scarab!

"Samma, Samma, Samma," said Scarab, "you sound just like Jobu. Why accept everything Jobu tells you as truth? You should question more and see the galaxy in a new, darker light!" Scarab gestured up to the sky. His face was scary, with red eyes wide, and a slight sneer on his lips.

"You lie, Scarab!" shouted Samma.

"Think what you want, child," said Scarab, "but the truth is much more complicated." Scarab turned back to Beatrice. "Your father didn't understand that by controlling the power buckets, we could help all aliens in the galaxy be equal. Think about it. Aliens from Mercury would be the same as aliens from Jupiter and Venus. No alien would have more than another alien. True equality!"

Then Scarab gestured toward Beatrice and looked at her locket. "Don't be like your father, Beatrice. Join me and together and we can—"

"*That's enough!*" came a strong voice from behind Beatrice. Everyone turned around to see Padinny, standing up tall, with a fierce look in her eyes. "I won't let you talk to my friends that way, *Father.*"

 eatrice's mouth fell open. "I knew it!" she thought to
 herself. Everything finally added up. Scarab was
Padinny's father!

Scarab appeared taken aback for a moment before regaining composure. "Why, hello, Padinny. I didn't see you there. It's been too long, my daughter."

"Not long enough!" shot back Padinny. Beatrice was very surprised. While she hadn't known Padinny that long, she had never seen her so angry!

Scarab seemed unshaken. "No need to get angry, Padinny. As much as I would love to catch up, I am here on official business."

"Yeah, to steal the power buckets!" shouted Padinny.

Scarab sighed. "You know, 'steal' is such a harsh term. Why don't we just say I am here to borrow them – forever!" Scarab and the Bracas all laughed.

Padinny was not amused.

Scarab looked at Padinny's fierce face. "My daughter, I know we have unfinished business, but now is not the time. If you and the POGs do not leave, then I will be forced to take matters in my own hands," and Scarab touched his gloves together, creating a huge ball of electricity that crackled in them.

"You know we can't do that, Scarab," said Keena. "Plus, I know how much you like to be beaten by a bunch of alien kids!"

Scarab smiled and started to laugh, snickering at first

then laughing harder and harder. All of a sudden, Scarab stopped laughing, and looked back at Beatrice, his eyes glancing at the locket around her neck. "Dear Beatrice, kindly give me your locket, and none of your friends need to get hurt."

Keena jumped up and yelled, "No way, Scarab! We are not afraid of—"

But before Keena could finish speaking, Scarab clapped his red gloves, and fired a lightning bolt at each of the POGs.

Before Beatrice could react, she felt herself being pushed over by Samma, falling hard onto the ground. Samma propped Beatrice up behind the boulder and said, "Stay here and let us handle this."

"Okay," managed Beatrice, as Samma quickly turned around and ran out from behind the boulder.

She peeked around the boulder to see the other POGs engaged in a battle with Scarab and the Bracas.

She saw Keena fire dozens of fireballs at a Braca who blocked them with an ice shield and then fired back small, black ice pellets. Keena dove behind a rock just in time to avoid the pellets striking him.

Cannie was chasing down a Braca by firing long ropes of ice that crashed down beside the Braca. "Take that, Braca!" yelled Cannie.

Padinny and Samma were engaged in a duel with two Bracas on the other side of the boulder. The Bracas shot ice missiles at them, which caused Padinny and Samma to take shelter under a large rock.

"They have the higher ground!" shouted Padinny. Turning to Samma, she smiled as she asked, "Can you get their attention for a few moments while I cook something up?"

"Sure thing!" Samma held up her hands and created a massive circle of gas that engulfed the Bracas, blinding them. Padinny then touched the stars on her chest and shot lightning bolts at the Bracas, who crashed to the ground under a pile of rocks.

"Nice!" shouted Padinny.

Beatrice sat there and felt powerless to help. She glanced over at Scarab and was amazed to see him just standing there with a smile on his face. *What was he up to?*

Meanwhile, Keena was engaged in a battle with a particularly large Braca. Just as Keena had the Braca cornered against the boulder, Scarab leapt into the air and flew over to where Keena was fighting. He held up one hand and produced a massive gust of wind that stopped Keena in his tracks. With his other hand, Scarab produced a small red box with a black button on top.

"Guys!" yelled Keena, suddenly more alarmed than before. "Careful, Scarab has a Red-Trap!"

Before anyone could react, Scarab pushed the black button on the Red-Trap, and Keena became ensnared inside a small red-lit cage. Keena was completely trapped, unable to help or fight. "How did he do that?" Beatrice thought to herself.

"No!" yelled Cannie, running over to try to help Keena. Cannie fired an ice missile at Scarab, who easily flew to the right, safely out of the way. Scarab once again hit the black button on the box, and just like that, Cannie was inside another Red-Trap.

"Rats!" yelled Cannie, slamming the inside of the cage with his hands. "Someone help us!"

Meanwhile, Samma and Padinny found themselves separated and fighting two Bracas on their own.

"We can do this, Padinny!" yelled Samma as she created a gas cloud in the air.

Padinny was conjuring everything she could think of, including lightning bolts, sleet, and even large gusts of wind.

Just then, Samma tripped and landed on the corner of the rocky ridge, surrounded by two Bracas and Scarab. Samma, breathing hard, looked up into the red eyes of Scarab.

"Samma," said Scarab, "I always appreciate a good fight. Sadly, today just isn't your day. You lose, Samma, you lose," and Scarab hit the black button. Now Samma found herself inside a Red-Trap.

"This isn't over, Scarab!" yelled Samma with a ferocious look in her eyes.

"Oh, but it is," replied Scarab with a laugh. "It is."

Scarab then turned his attention to Padinny, who had been captured and was standing there, being held by the four Bracas.

"My sweet, sweet daughter," began Scarab.

But Padinny cut him off, "Do *not* call me that. You do not have the right to call me 'daughter.' Free my friends and we can talk!"

"Talk?" snickered Scarab. "You think I came here to talk? We have done enough talking!" and Scarab hit a different button on his box. Red ropes flew out of the box and tied themselves around Padinny's arms and legs.

Another rope tied itself around Padinny's mouth, making it impossible for her to speak.

"There," said a relieved Scarab, "that's much better." The Bracas all smiled.

Scarab put the box away in his pocket and turned his attention to Beatrice. She sat there beside the boulder, trembling in fear.

"Hello again, Beatrice," said Scarab, slightly out of breath. He wiped some sweat off his brow and said, "As I mentioned earlier, I believe you have something that belongs to me," gesturing to the locket.

Beatrice didn't know what to do. She looked around and saw her friends stuck in Red-Traps, unable to help her. She was alone and very scared. But then she thought about something her dad had said about the locket:

"...it's been known to help in times of need."

Beatrice thought for a second. This was definitely a time of need! She stood up from beside the boulder, looked Scarab straight in his red eyes, and said in a strong voice she didn't know she had, "No, Scarab. I will not give you the locket. Not now and not ever!"

Samma and Keena exchanged worried glances.

Scarab clapped and clapped, mocking Beatrice. "Oh, how I applaud your bravery. But, my child, you have no choice," replied Scarab as he walked closer and closer to where Beatrice was standing. Scarab's gloves began to glow, and he shot a lightning bolt that struck the ground right beside Beatrice.

"Ouch!" Beatrice yelled out, more in shock than pain.

Padinny tried to scream but couldn't be heard through the red ropes covering her mouth.

Scarab laughed and laughed. "What's that, daughter?" joked Scarab as he gestured over to where Padinny was trapped.

"Give up, Beatrice," said Scarab. "There is nothing you can do." Scarab raised his arms and dumped a pile of ice pellets on Beatrice's head.

Beatrice yelped in surprise and raised her hands to cover her head to avoid the cold ice. In doing so, her hand accidentally rubbed against the orange locket.

Samma screamed, "Stop it, Scarab!"

"But I can't, Jobu Junior!" joked Scarab. The Bracas laughed.

Beatrice felt a warm feeling on her chest and glanced down to see that her locket had started to glow.

"Let's dance, Beatrice!" Scarab said as he shot lightning bolts on each side of Beatrice, causing her to jump back and forth.

It was clear he was playing with her, having fun at her expense. Keena and Cannie looked defeated. Samma looked worried. Padinny looked angry.

While Scarab was showing off to everyone, Beatrice glanced down and noticed her locket glowing brighter and brighter. She covered it with her other hand. Beatrice realized she had to hide her locket because if Scarab saw it glowing, he might hurt Beatrice and her friends in his attempt to steal it.

But it was too late. Scarab stopped and looked directly at Beatrice. "Child, enough of these games. Just hand the locket over and I will let all of your friends go." He gave a mocking smile. "I am feeling particularly generous today."

Beatrice just stared back at Scarab without blinking.

Scarab glared at Beatrice. "Four friends for one locket. Take the deal, Beatrice, or I am going to have to use more—well...creative methods," Scarab said and looked down at his gloves, which were burning with electricity.

Beatrice stared at Scarab then looked over at her friends. She felt the locket against her chest and in that moment, something changed inside her. All of her fear vanished; she felt brave, warm, confident, and in control. Better than that, she knew what she had to do.

"Okay, Scarab," she said in a clear, unwavering voice. "You win."

Samma's eyes widened. "Beatrice, what are you doing?"

"Don't give it to him!" shouted Keena.

But Beatrice shrugged off her friends. She turned back to Scarab and took a few steps closer to him.

"The locket is all yours." Beatrice cupped the locket in both of her hands, hiding the glow from Scarab. She gently held her hands out from her body and pointed them in Scarab's direction. "Just come get it."

Scarab let out a sigh of relief, relaxed his shoulders, and smiled. "Thank you, Beatrice. I am so happy to hear that."

"What about my friends?" said Beatrice, still cupping the locket in her hands.

"A deal is a deal, my dear. As soon as I get the locket, your friends will be freed." Scarab approached Beatrice and stood about two feet from her. "Now give me the locket."

Beatrice looked closely at Scarab. She had never been this close to him, and to be honest, she wasn't impressed. He looked old, scared, and tired. She gave a laugh.

Scarab looked confused. "What's so funny?"

Beatrice stopped laughing and looked Scarab straight in the eyes. "I'm sorry, but you just aren't as scary as I thought you'd be."

"What?" asked a confused Scarab.

Beatrice went on. "Did you really think that I would believe you'd free the POGs? No way, Scarab."

Samma looked alarmed and glanced over to Keena. "What is going on?"

Scarab just stood there.

"To be honest," said Beatrice, "I feel really good, better than ever. I feel relieved. I feel free. I feel myself."

"Enough of this," said Scarab, with a slight catch in his voice. "As much as I would love to hear about your personal journey, please hand over the locket." Scarab reached his hand out so it was just in front of Beatrice.

As quickly as she could, Beatrice removed her hands from the locket and thrust her chest out toward Scarab. A huge beam of bright, white light shot out of Beatrice's locket at Scarab, striking him squarely in the chest.

Scarab had no time to react. "*Ahhhh*!" he yelled, falling backward, trapped in the beam of the light. The fall caused him to drop the box used to control the Red-Traps. Beatrice quickly reached down, grabbed the box, and hit the black button on top.

The Red-Traps immediately disappeared, and the POGs were freed, catching the Bracas off guard. Keena and Cannie shot to attention and launched a barrage of fireballs and ice pellets in the direction of the Bracas. The Bracas ran for cover beside the boulder in an attempt to regroup.

Meanwhile, Scarab lay trapped in the beam of light. As he lay there unable to move, an orange light emerged from Scarab's chest. The light displayed a hologram that looked very similar to the map of the Power Buckets from Beatrice's locket. To Beatrice's surprise, the words at the top of the map didn't say *MAP OF POWER BUCKETS*, but instead read *MAP OF LOCKETS*.

Padinny quickly realized what had happened and took a picture of the map with her POG-Watch. As the POGs retreated from Scarab and the Bracas, Beatrice stood there holding the beam of light firmly affixed to Scarab's chest.

"Don't just stand there!" shouted Scarab to the other Bracas, grimacing under the pressure of the light, "Do something!"

The Bracas turned their attention from the retreating

POGs to Beatrice, firing ice pellets at her.

"Ouch!" shouted Beatrice as the ice rained down over her head, but she stood firm. "Run, guys! I don't know how much longer I can hold it!"

Samma stopped and turned toward Beatrice, "We can't leave you, Beatrice!"

But Beatrice shook her head. "If this is how I can help, then let me help. Go back to Jobu, tell the POGs everything, and go after the lockets! The lockets are the key to stopping Scarab and the Bracas forever!"

Before Samma could argue, a giant ice missile crashed down beside her, causing her to fall backward. "Okay, Beatrice, but hold on! We will radio for help once we get back to the spaceship!" Samma ran back to Cannie, Keena, and Padinny, and the POGs disappeared into the distance, safely on their way back to the other POGs, the spaceship, SEAK, and Jobu.

Once she saw her friends had safely escaped, Beatrice closed the locket, collapsing onto the ground in exhaustion. The Bracas flew over and surrounded her.

Scarab, looking a bit dazed, quickly stood up and turned to Beatrice. He was breathing hard and wiped the dust from his cape. "You, child, are proving more of a menace than I thought possible! How did you control *my* locket like that?!"

"Your locket?" asked Beatrice with a sly grin on her face. "I don't know, Scarab. Maybe *my* locket just doesn't like you!"

Scarab's face went from mean to meaner. "You will pay for this!" he yelled, raising his arms high above his body, creating a large ball of electricity with his red gloves.

As Scarab got ready to fire, Beatrice sat there calmly with a contented smile on her face. She wasn't scared! No matter what happened, Beatrice was happy she had helped her friends escape so they could protect the galaxy. It had certainly been a strange birthday, but she wouldn't trade it for anything in the world – or galaxy!

As Scarab readied to shoot at Beatrice, an orange beam of light struck him squarely on the arm, causing him to drop the ball of electricity and stumble backward.

"What?!" he yelled out in disbelief.

Beatrice, Scarab, and the Bracas turned to see Jobu standing next to another alien who was wearing a mask. The two of them stood there, bravely facing Scarab and the Bracas.

"Jobu!" cried out Beatrice in relief.

"Hello, my dear," replied Jobu. "Are you all right?"

"Yes, I'm fine," said Beatrice, staring at the other alien. *Who was with Jobu? Had there been another alien at SEAK that she hadn't met?*

"It's nice to see you, old friend," Jobu called out to Scarab in a cynical tone.

Scarab glared at Jobu. "Why hello, Jobu. Oh, how I have missed you and your little POGs. Who's your little friend?" Scarab gestured to the alien standing beside Jobu. Scarab furrowed his brow and said, "You look familiar. Do I know you?"

Nothing could have prepared Beatrice for what happened next.

The other alien removed his mask, and Beatrice gasped. There, in beat-up sneakers, shorts, and a green t-shirt, stood her father.

Dad

ad!" she blurted out.

"Hi, my dear," said her dad in the same calm and friendly voice he used when he asked what she wanted for breakfast.

"What's going on?!" Beatrice thought to herself.

"Dad, what are you doing here?" Beatrice blurted out. "How did you get here? Where is Mom?!"

Beatrice's dad held up his hand. "I know you have questions, sweetie, but right now I have to deal with an old friend."

Beatrice's dad turned to Scarab, who stood there with a mean scowl on his face. "Scarab, old friend, it seems that we have some unfinished business."

Scarab didn't reply. He just stood there, glaring at Beatrice's dad.

Beatrice's dad went on. "Jobu and I are here to end your reign of fear. No longer shall you control the aliens in our galaxy. No longer shall the Bracas steal power buckets from innocent, hard-working aliens."

Scarab yelled out, "Oh, spare me the boring lecture. What do *you* think you can do about it, anyway?"

Beatrice's dad smiled and said nothing. He reached down and grabbed hold of his wedding ring. The silver band of the ring began to blink, and the ground began to shake! All of a sudden, *crash!* The ground cracked, and fire rushed to the surface. The Bracas were taken by surprise and forced to fly high up into the air, away from the fiery ground below. Jobu pushed a button on her suit, and she flew up into the air after the Bracas, firing shot after shot of hot lava at them.

Scarab, now separated from his team and caught completely off guard, leapt into the air and fired a few lightning bolts at Beatrice's dad, which were easily deflected. Seeing that his options were limited, Scarab flew high up into the air after Jobu and the Bracas.

Beatrice's dad waited until Scarab had flown out of sight. Then he let go of his wedding band, and everything became still again. He walked over to Beatrice and hugged her tightly.

Beatrice didn't know what to do or say. What had just happened?

Her dad spoke first. "Well, hi there, my dear." He paused for a few seconds. "Umm, welcome to Mercury!" He gestured around him and gave a big smile.

Beatrice was not amused and stared at her dad. "Dad," she began.

But Beatrice's dad interrupted. "Yes, we have lots to talk about. There is so much I have wanted to tell you."

"Then tell me!" yelled Beatrice.

Beatrice's dad sighed. "I will, I will. I promise that I will tell you everything, but right now I need to help Jobu and chase after Scarab and the Bracas. It's part of our plan."

"What plan?" asked Beatrice.

"Jobu's plan to get the lockets back. If Jobu and I can keep Scarab on the run, then you and the POGs can go collect the lockets using the coordinates Padinny copied down."

"How are you going to do that?" asked Beatrice, standing back from her dad and folding her arms. "Scarab is so powerful. What if something happens to you? What do I tell Mom? Wait—does she know?!"

Beatrice's dad listened patiently and said with a smile, "I will tell you everything. I promise." He pulled Beatrice in for a hug and kissed the top of her head. "I love you, my dear. Be safe and believe in yourself. I will see you soon!" Beatrice's dad pulled back, pushed a few buttons on his watch, and put his mask back on.

Beatrice gave a little sniffle. "Promise me you'll be okay, Dad."

"I promise!" he said as he flew off the ground. "Focus on the mission. Jobu and I will keep Scarab away, so you can collect the lockets and save the galaxy." He blew Beatrice a kiss, turned in the air, and flew off into the distance.

Beatrice watched and watched until she couldn't see him anymore. Tears streamed down her face. She turned to walk back to the spaceship. There in front of her stood all of the POGs, smiling and waving.

eatrice!" shouted Rala.

"You were amazing!" exclaimed Cannie.

Padinny said nothing. She just ran up and gave Beatrice a big hug.

One by one, the other POGs came over to congratulate Beatrice. When it was Jana's turn, Beatrice got nervous. Jana just stood there with a cold look on her face, peering at Beatrice with dark blue and beady eyes.

"You," she began before bursting into a big smile and turning her eyes light blue, "are all right with me!" Beatrice exhaled, feeling relieved. "But I'm still watching you!" joked Jana with a laugh.

Beatrice felt safe. She was where she needed to be.

"What now?" she finally said.

Samma answered. "Now we have a plan. Thanks to Beatrice, we have exact locations for six lockets. While Jobu and Beatrice's father keep Scarab and the Bracas at bay, we can go collect the lockets and bring them back to SEAK for safekeeping. This is a dangerous mission, but we can do it, POGs!"

"Sounds good to me!" said Keena. "Let's go!"

"Yahoo!" shouted Graniten.

"Wait, six lockets?" asked Beatrice. "With mine that makes only seven. Where is the last locket?"

Samma pointed up to the sky. "It's around Scarab's neck."

"I was afraid of that," said Beatrice. "How can we possibly get his locket?"

Before Samma could answer, Padinny interrupted and said confidently, "Leave that to me."

Beatrice smiled and put her arm around Padinny's shoulder. "How about we do it together?"

The POGs walked back to the spaceship, talking and laughing with one another. Beatrice turned to look one last time at Mercury's beautiful, fiery landscape. She didn't know if or when she'd be back, but she knew that she would never forget this adventure or the adventures that were soon to come.

Cory Hills

Percussionist, composer, and storyteller Cory Hills is the creator of Percussive Storytelling, a program that brings classical music and storytelling to kids in fun and accessible ways. The program recently marked its 470th performance, and has reached more than 110,000 children in eight countries.

The Lost Bicycle, Hills' debut solo CD of percussive stories, has received four national parenting and creative arts awards (NAPPA Parent's Awards Gold, Parent's Choice Award Silver, World Storytelling Honors Award, and a Creative Child preferred choice). In June 2015, The Lost Bicycle was released as a fully illustrated children's book published by AcutebyDesign. In 2016, Hills released his second album of percussive stories called Drum Factory, on Sono Luminus Records. Drum Factory received a Parent's Choice Silver Award, three nominations at the 2016 Independent Music Awards, and was named CD of Year by Creative Child.

Hills has degrees from Northwestern University, Queensland Conservatorium, and the University of Kansas, and was awarded a research fellowship to Institute Fabrica. Currently, Hills is an active performer and recording artist in Los Angeles, as well as a member of the Grammy-nominated Los Angeles Percussion Quartet.

For more information, please visit www.splatboombang.com.

Jane Elliott *explores the world of art making through various mediums, including drawing, painting, photography, metal sculpting, woodworking, costume making, and surface pattern design. She is especially inspired by graphic novels - as a child she was fascinated by books of wallpaper samples and bolts of fabric. Working in her studio she produces shadowbox art, collage works, and watercolor paintings.*

Elliot received a degree in visual art from Cal State Fullerton and currently resides in San Francisco above a delicious Italian Deli alongside her tenor saxophone named Athena.